Solutions 2

Solutions 2

Daylight on America's Dark Side
Pandering Politics, Loss and
How to Change Course

Author of *Pondering Alphabetic Solutions* and *No Land an Island*

Dr. Carolyn LaDelle Bennett

Print information available on the last page.

To order additional copies of this book, contact:
Xlibris
1-888-795-4274
www.Xlibris.com
Orders@Xlibris.com
766176

CONTENTS

TIME OUT

CONSIDER WORDS AND DEMEANOR

No more "we are shocked" and "our thoughts and prayers"
for families of another US mass shooting
No more massacres and maiming of
Afghan, Iraqi, Libyan, Pakistani, Somali, Sudanese, Syrian, Yemeni
children felled by US bombs

Dedication
to
nonviolence
honored values of
life, sovereignty, self-determination of all peoples
To those courageous enough to live these principles

ACKNOWLEDGMENTS

I offer my sincere appreciation to the staff, consultants and associates in manuscript submission, copyediting, indexing, design, production and publishing at Xlibris and Author Solutions. As author of *Solutions 2*, I take full responsibility for my work.

FIRST WORDS

DAYLIGHT LAYS BARE the unacceptable accepted, a glorified, lauded network of entitled corruption, counterfeit values and priorities, and collective deceit—the dark side of US officialdom and entanglements—which are destroying the United States of America, World nations and peoples, Society as a Whole, and the Universe.

Solutions 2 seeks a change of mind and methods; a change of language, attitude, and approach; a change of principles and of character, concern, competency, and performance in the public (the people) and public officials, in the print and broadcast press. *Solutions 2* seeks substantive change in the caliber and course of US foreign and domestic relations.

The state of the nation is neither strong nor courageous but is in a seriously weakened state brought on by toxic elements rising from the dark side. These toxic elements include scaremongering, mind control, manipulation, meanness, maintenance of the disease of violence, madness produced and directed by pimping moguls and pandering politicians, media *misinformants* revolving in and out of government, propaganda mills, think tanks, and sundry industries in a cult of pandering politics that drives peoples and nations against one another—against their common humanity, society, and solidarity—and toward physical, social, psychological, and political cannibalism and annihilation. This is the true state of a divided nation, the United States of America, and the state of the world in the post–World War II era under corrupt, criminal, cowardly, incompetent leadership staggering in an anachronistic quest, not for goodness but for world dominance.

The great challenge before the world—our mission as peoples of the world—is to come together in sustained, nonviolent efforts intent on changing our sensibility toward and conception and understanding of the world and intent on changing the character, the leading cast, and the course of history.

I write this book as an American and from the vantage point of my homeland but also with an international perspective and a keen sense of history. As the author of earlier works, *No Land an Island: No People Apart* and *Pondering Alphabetic Solutions*, I continue to set out some of a course of study that sheds light on the critical state of US-led world and national affairs and its consequences; and to offer solutions concerning the quality of citizenry, government, and media.

In this offering, I hope I have been as civil and respectful as I wish others would be. I hope I have refrained from abusing or misusing language, using language slanderously to libel, malign, or smear, or in ways that reflect negatively not only on me (the speaker) but on the representation and standing of the nation represented (as has been done in reckless high-profile performances of such US public officials as Hillary Rodham Clinton, Susan Rice, Victoria Nuland, Samantha Power, and Nikki Haley). I hope I have homed in on basic principles to consider in crafting solutions: share and share alike. There is equality in sharing, not as charity, which is, in reality, condescension, pity, and noblesse oblige, which means one is obliged not as equal but as innate superior to innate inferior—superiority that, as it condescends with charity, entitles itself to plunder, to threaten, to take the land and natural resources of others, and to destroy all who dissent or resist.

I hope I have harmed no one in either speech or attitude. I hope my pronouns do not misrepresent my intent. I speak for myself, and though I, too, fall into the *we* (*us, our*) usage, I prefer not to, as I can speak for no one except myself. I am not attached to "royalty," and the royal *we* rings neither royal nor authentic. I hope I have spoken persuasively of the crisis in the United States' standing in the world and the crisis surrounding the loss of trust in institutions of media, press, government, schooling, and law at home and abroad. I hope I have driven home the imperative of establishing and restoring trust, deepening essential honor and honesty, and establishing and maintaining credibility and accountability, competence and professionalism, and unselfish service to society and the common good.

I hope I have illustrated the critical connection between *violence* and *violence*, whether on the streets of America; on the journey taken by remote missiles that rain down on the peoples of Afghanistan, Iraq, Syria, Pakistan, and Somalia; or through the verbal threats and provocations lodged against Russia, Turkey, Iran, and Korea. The volatility of US leadership, US. nuclear might, and nearly seventy years of occupation have presented an ongoing threat to both the Democratic People's Republic of Korea and the Republic of Korea (North and South Korea), and to their northern neighbors, the People's Republic of China and the Russian Federation. Ordinary people unencumbered by extreme partisanship, nationalism, tribalism, and other isms surely see that the endless reign of violence, on all fronts, must end.

I have highlighted the nature of our (America's) true values, evidenced in the actions, demeanor, policies, and practices of our (US) leaders (we *are* what we do); the connection between priorities and values; and the domestic and international consequences that attend thereto. US violence abroad *is* violence against the homeland.

In 2017, the United Nations Special Rapporteur on extreme poverty and human rights, Professor Philip Alston, concluded a fact-finding investigation of conditions in the United States and issued a report. In a published statement, he said that Americans he interviewed recited glowingly, as a mantra, the notion of "American 'exceptionalism.'" But the images and conditions on the ground revealed an America that, instead of realizing the "admirable commitments" of America's founders, has proved itself "to be exceptional in far more problematic ways that are shockingly at odds with its immense wealth and its founding commitment to human rights."

The Reverend Dr. Joan B. Campbell wrote of an America in the 1960s that, sadly, reflects conditions in present-day America. "However benevolent and kind we might wish to be" (or we might tell the world we are), she said, the violence that surrounds us "in our streets and in our homes and in our world" speaks the reality—"that we have succumbed to the temptation of the desert. We face a deep and profound spiritual crisis."

I hope I have offered nonviolent alternatives. I hope I have kept the focus on ideas, issues, and principles, not on personalities. Personalities are passing. Principles are everlasting.

PROBLEM

Corruption, Manipulation, Destructiveness Undermining Society, Common Good

[A] single injustice, a single crime, a single illegality, particularly if it is . . . confirmed, a single wrong to humanity, a single wrong to justice and to right, particularly if it is universally, legally, nationally, commodiously accepted—that single crime shatters and is sufficient to shatter the whole social pact, the whole social contract . . . [That single crime], a single dishonorable act [brings] about the loss of one's honor, the dishonor of a whole people. It is a touch of gangrene that corrupts the entire body.
—French poet Charles-Pierre Péguy (1873–1914)
in *Respectfully Quoted* (quote 958, page 184)

Pandering Politics

It happens every day . . . : a lobbyist calls the majority leader, the minority leader, the speaker; some chairmen or ranking member gets a call saying, "hey go light on that." That kind of influence goes on. Anyone who says it doesn't hasn't been in the position I've been in.

—Hon. Darrel Issa
Member of the US House of Representatives
(January 3, 2001–2018)
Committee on Oversight and
Government Reform chairman

PANDERING IS LIKE prostitution—only worse! In the interest of personal gain, nothing is sacred. Anything and everything is up for grabs. Everything of real, substantive value is sacrificed, thrown to the curb, discarded, given up for the self-serving benefit of panderers. Institutions break down, basic laws are broken, human rights are abused, and human relations are severed; interaction, civil engagement, discussion, conversation, and dissent are abandoned, denied, or disparaged as weakness, lacking in chauvinist bluster.

Whole nations and peoples are destroyed. Heads of state and other foreign leaders are assassinated, their lives taken, and their reputations ruined as the panderers get rich and entrench their power by pandering to passing fads, private and often strange preferences, and/or momentary, expedient alliances. The servant of private individuals and quite often individuals holding public office, pandering politics aids nothing of the public or the common good. Contrary to the conventional wisdom, it is not the office that corrupts but individuals who corrupt office. It is not government that is corrupt but panderers and corrupt government officials who corrupt government. Just as these destroyers ruin the lives and reputations of other individuals, foreign and domestic—their reach extending from gerrymandered local communities to tiny islands in the Pacific and the farthest places on the globe—they also destroy the institution of law and other essential institutions that should serve sovereignty and the body politic. They poison society, sacrifice public trust, and ultimately destroy society itself.

Well positioned within the United States of America are cabals, interlocking cabals that corrupt corruptible officials who pander to the wishes of cabal CEOs and others. No person can be coerced into breaking the law or coerced into betraying public trust without his or her choosing to betray public trust, choosing to lie, cheat, and steal. Membership in the cult of pandering politics includes such areas as medical and pharmaceutical businesses, huge industries such as weapons industries, professions of various kinds, institutions such as universities, religions, sundry NGOs, nonprofits and not-for-profits, and think tanks whose wishes public officials pander for their own profit. It is no accident that public officials who revolve in and out of government "service" (self-service) or remain entrenched for life in government "service" (service to themselves) get a whole lot richer while inside than on first entry. Pandering maintains a self-interested status quo and denies the good that would bring health to the whole.

On January 20, 2017, the incoming president of the United States remarked that for many years, Federal Washington, politicians, and a "small group"—but not the masses of Americans—have triumphed. "The establishment," he said, has "protected itself, but not the citizens of America." In his inaugural speech, President Donald J. Trump accurately observed that "Washington [had] flourished," but the people "did not share in its wealth." Politicians prospered, but "jobs left" and "factories closed." Among the many, he said, there has been little to celebrate: "Mothers and children [are] trapped in poverty in our inner cities, rusted-out factories [are] scattered like tombstones across the landscape of our nation, an education system flush with cash [has left] our young and beautiful students deprived of knowledge, crime and gangs and drugs . . . have stolen too many lives and robbed our country of . . . much unrealized potential. . . . For too long, a small group . . . has reaped the rewards of government while the people have borne the cost." Truth spoken awaits cooperative concrete solutions, but the nation is served with infighting, distraction, and a status quo of pandering politics.

Society, Self-Undone

Pandering concentrates power and entrenches denial, normalizing what is anything but normal. Pandering militates against society, prevents its healthy functioning, and ultimately causes its breakdown. It is also the constant driver of corruption among individuals in high office. As public "servants" are compromised by their industry paymasters, diseases are not cured but sustained; depression is not removed but drugged. The United States boasts a failed public health system, multiple varieties of drug and disease epidemics, and more than fifty years of war and interference in countries boasting huge plantation sources from which addictive drugs derive (Afghanistan's poppy fields, South America's coca orchards becoming narcotics and knockoffs or synthetics). Now epidemic in the USA, opioid, or opiate 1a, is a synthetic drug with narcotic properties and, though not derived from opium (poppy seeds), is similar to opiate drugs, such as morphine or codeine, which derive from or contain opium. From the South American coca shrub comes the highly addictive cocaine. From Afghanistan, Britain, Germany, and Eurasia comes heroin, the *most highly addictive* narcotic, first synthesized from morphine (opium) by a British chemist in 1874 and introduced as a commercial product by the Bayer Company in 1898. Also in demand in the US marketplace is Ecstasy (a.k.a. MDMA), a hallucinogenic-propertied synthetic of the amphetamine family of drugs. The present situation of panderers and masters begs the question not of a Trump-Russia collusion but of collusions and conspiracies of another kind; and with whom, in support of which war, against whom? On this apparent journey of self-annihilation—who wins and who loses?

In calling to mind another president's words, George Monbiot wrote, "The liberty of a democracy is not safe if the people tolerate the growth of private power to a point where it becomes stronger than their democratic state itself." Through bloodletting, propaganda, tyranny, and misinformation overload, US leaders are busy "exporting democracy" to other countries and simultaneously destroying any residue or promise of democratic process within the United States.

In his February 2017 article, Monbiot recalls that "soon after the second world war," some of the richest people in America began "setting up a network of think tanks" purporting to offer "dispassionate opinions on public affairs," but in fact, they were designed to promote their own private interests. They were "more like corporate lobbyists, working on behalf of those who fund them." Down to the present day, and long before now–US President Donald Trump campaigned for or won the US presidency, campaign funding in the United States "had systematically corrupted the political system." Big money pays. It pays for exposure. It buys campaigns and public officials. And those who take the money and other perks kick back what their masters expect of them. In the past thirty years, Monbiot reports, "corporate donors have come to dominate" campaign funding. George Monbiot's thoughts are absolutely correct as far as they go, but the damage extends further than a "democracy," however defined.

The construct of society is greater and should be given greater consideration than governments, political processes, or ideologies. Consequences of the deepening normalization of corruption extend to the whole society, local to global; and within the United States, the origins of corruption extend to members of both major *tyrannical* political parties. These parties, Patrick Martin wrote in early January 2017, are "political instrument[s] of billionaires." Each party is a mere variation on a singular theme: At one moment, a party adopts a self-serving McCarthy era "anti-Russian stance" and aligns "more closely with the military-intelligence apparatus." But both major US political parties are endorsers of the decades-long "ever-increasing concentration of wealth" and the "crystallization of a semi-criminal ruling class whose wealth" derives *not* "from the development of the productive forces" but from "financial manipulation."

No tribe or insignia of entrenched power brokers, no politicians or partners or wannabes are excluded from card-carrying membership in the cult of pay-to-play criminals in breach of public trust. "In years past," Whitney Webb reported at *MintPress News*, the Arkansas-born state governor (1979–1981, 1983–1992) and forty-second US president and his Chicago-born bride formed a foundation that has raked in "significant donations from individuals and countries that sought to purchase influence in Washington." Following their example, the Panama-born US senior senator representing Arizona formed the McCain Institute and began raking in "large sums from the likes of George Soros and Saudi Arabia" (the former was reportedly notorious for "fomenting coups and buying elections around the world"; the latter was implicated in the 2001 US-based World Trade Center disaster and, in 2017 and 2018, aided by US military sales and service support, was involved in decimating the land and people of the Aden Gulf coastal country of Yemen, one of the poorest countries in the world).

The cashing-in cult membership moves from America's southwest eastward to former US vice president Joe Biden (together with his president), who also revolves from government into book publishing and circuit lecturing funneled (or laundered) through a new foundation. Politician Biden, Phil Butler wrote in April of 2017, left a legacy that "feathered the beds of the upper-middle class and the ultimate elites," and the lower classes "fleeced once again." At the federal government level, the legacy of debt "more than doubled . . . as pork barrel and military spending bailed out only big finance." The Obama-Biden tenure saw corporate profits rise "to 144 percent over previous wins, while home ownership and other key metrics for most Americans fell dramatically." On their watch, "the richest country on Earth" hosted "36 percent more people" than during the previous administration on stamps for food. Butler concluded that the admin team of 2008–2016 "brought nothing but more misery" to Americans subsisting on the lowest income. The legacy was "a socio-economic piñata with deadly candies tucked away inside." And the games of persons in power continued.

Pay to Play, Pay to Stay

Everything's for sale, even US citizenship. Individually and as a body, members of the US legislature have long been in violation of the federal oath of office, having sold themselves and their services and permitted the selling off of the essential public sector, public space, and public interest to private interests and profiteers. Added to these egregious acts is the selling (and acquiescence to the selling) of US citizenship.

The buyers are powerful private corporate and individual interests, and the relatively new White House occupants with sundry partners and associates have reportedly upped the ante. A federal program tagged EB-5 reportedly authorizes the going price of wealthy family visas at $500,000 a clip (CIS). On August 1, 2016, *the Washington Examiner* reported that "the E-2 and EB-5 are two of the most notoriously abused visa categories that essentially allow wealthy foreigners to buy their way to U.S. residency, and possibly citizenship, with a relatively modest investment" (*Examiner* quoting Center for Immigration Studies policy director Jessica Vaughan). The August 1, 2016, news article by Paul Bedard focuses on Khizr M. Khan, an "immigration lawyer specializing in a 'highly controversial' program" that has been "accused of letting immigrants buy their way" into the United States.

The event in a *Washington Examiner* report by Kyle Feldscher (May 6, 2017) is said to be billed the "golden" $500,000-a-clip US visa: "Invest $500,000 and immigrate to the United States," an event closed to journalists who, if caught, risk being "tossed out" of a hall where the sister of U.S. President Donald Trump's son-in-law urges "Chinese investors in Beijing to pump money into her family's business in order to receive a visa to the United States." Her presentation reportedly includes "hours of slideshows and presentations from representatives of the Kushners' family business." Reportedly "among the pitches was one promising that investing hundreds of thousands of dollars in a Kushner project could lead to receiving an EB-5 immigrant investor visa, known in China as the 'golden visa.'" Tolerating the selling of citizenship and/or the banning of press coverage is another example of US members of congress's pandering to private interest and prostituting their office, instead of doing their jobs under law as representatives on behalf of the United States of America, its people, and the common good.

The implied message in schemes such as the golden $500,000 seems to be that victims of US invasions or poor people need not apply. Under US Department of Homeland Security management, with "DHS-licensed regional centers" (CIS) handling the investments, it seems that part of the EB-5 program "allows an 'alien' investor with no other qualifications to secure a set of green cards" for a family that includes "the investor, the investor's spouse, and all their under 21-years-of-age [offspring] if $500,000 is invested in a Department of Homeland Security–approved, non-guaranteed investment." The program might be described as chain migration for the half-million-USD set. The reach of corruption and abuse of power seems boundless, unchecked, and beyond moral or ethical principle.

Pandering Politics' Reach and Ramifications

As it generates or produces a *normalization* of harm, pandering is, by any standard, devoid of principle. Principled behavior is behavior that is characterized by or based on some "comprehensive and fundamental law, doctrine, rule or code of conduct" (edited from Merriam-Webster)—principle of a *good* sort. Hence, a *great* nation, in my view, must be a good nation. This is slightly different from the US president's borrowed words, "the state of our Union is strong because our people are strong." Though it is unclear what the president meant by *strong*, it is not enough, even from a president who promised to make "America 'great' again." Thus, a nation is as great and/or as strong as it is good; it is as great and as strong as its people are good. Pandering is not an act of goodness.

Pandering means catering to or exploiting the weaknesses of others, providing gratification for others' desires; acting as a go-between, as does a pimp, who, by definition, makes use of others and/or conditions, often dishonorably, to gain or benefit personally. Politicians who pander to and pimp their offices for war industrialists, weapons makers, and traders on the pretext that they are providing for Americans' security or, in their words, "keeping America safe" are really engaged in feeding the war machine's insatiable appetite for endless wars, creating a cycle of hostility, violence, and conflict that makes no country safe, no country secure. These deadly, deceitful politicians are the most dangerous. They sacrifice principle to violence. To enrich themselves, they destroy, without qualm, Americans and other nationals. They constitute a threat to the whole world. Pandering politics and politicians threaten the world and are often joined by another layer of citizens who, following big power's example, though on a smaller scale, cash in by gaming the system.

Gamers and panderers. Pandering politicians in search of an election-day edge make strange bedfellows with people who insist on seating their pet peacocks on US flight 123 (not a real flight name and number)—the "gamers" of the system. Examples of pandering to gamers of the system are those who push wildlife or animals where animals should not be, to comfort gamers' feigned illnesses. They are sex-altering gamers who would breach fundamental societal parameters and demand public responsibility and/or financing of a purely personal decision to make physiological changes in their body. They are gamers who decide whether or not, when, and how to have children, and politicians who agree by drafting policy and allotting public funds for purely personal matters.

Assisting the blind and the deaf are matters of State, civil rights enabling people to be fully functional or as functional as possible. Animal assistance for subjectively determined emotional problems is not a matter of State; nor are conditions of sex alterations or personal matters of reproduction. These are personal and individual decisions, personal desires, not matters of civil rights or rights under law. There is no right to sex change or any personal desire.

Matters falling in the category of fundamental or universal rights are rights to food, clean water, clean air, sanitation, decent work, and permanent shelter (not homeless shelters or "house" boxes on streets or under bridges);

these are basic rights owed human beings as human beings and are to be protected by the State. It seems ludicrous, even immoral, to watch people languishing in homelessness while others have the luxuries of changing their sex paid for by the public treasury. The latter is often promoted by politicians pandering to a certain segment of society, while principled leadership would see State interest and society's benefit in enabling homeless people to be self-sufficient. Human beings and the State have a stake, an absolute interest in, and a natural concern for the basic health of society, society's people, and their ability to contribute to society. A great nation and good leaders understand the difference between essential rights and luxury, the distinction between matters in which the State has a legitimate stake and where it has not; and they act accordingly. But we are hard-pressed to find such independent leaders, as indicated by the pandering disestablishment of public schooling.

Schooling and panderers. Pandering to sects, segregationists, or separatists has virtually destroyed the common school and its original purpose to properly ensure our Union: to appropriately enculturate the young and embrace the immigrant, sowing good seeds that will flower into good, contributing citizens. Too many graduates of US K-12 schools, even those born in the United States, are noticeably deficient in self-discipline and reflective thought and are barely literate and insufficiently fluent in the language of their homeland, the country that gave them birth.

Not only are separatists' schools questionable in essential quality and standards, but in their parochialism, their narrowness, they also rob primary- and secondary-level schooling of its essential mission of teaching social skills and discipline (in course work and behavior) to the young in their formative years. The essentials include providing experiences for healthy exposure to and interaction with varieties of people in school-age groups; teaching the basics not only of language and calculating but also of freedom in creation, imagination, innovation (a discipline that yields independence of thought); offering a healthy enculturation into the United States of America together with a fair knowledge and appreciation of world geography and varieties of countries, cultures, and peoples.

Pandering lowers educational standards and the quality of teaching and learning, all the while claiming to improve these. It divides by pitting homeschooling, segregated academies, and charter schools against public schools or common schools where pupils learn academic basics, including the language and subject matter of their common country, civics, history, documents, and how to interact and get along with different kinds of people of one nation that is, in fact, indivisible.

The legitimate process by which individuals learn the traditional content of a culture and assimilate its practices and values, *enculturation*, should not be a bad word or authority's abuse. It should not be done carelessly or with insensibility, incivility, or violence, but as a means of sharing what makes many one; and in the process inviting the young, whether newer or older immigrant, on an exciting journey of growth and development. Curricular content of enculturation should include civics and geography and natural places, grammatically correct written and spoken English usage, and discussion and debate without slang or profanity. Content should be taught without exaggeration or arrogance but basically, truly, and humbly, with the certain knowledge that immigrants, too, have migrated from great and authentic cultures that may be in various stages of development, often having been tormented, plundered, and stymied in their development by Western nations, yet having survived for far more years than the United States of America. The content of enculturation should not be taught by ideologues, dogmatists or the narrow-minded; nor should it include propaganda or the promulgation of fantasies such as US exceptionalism and Manifest Destiny (entitled and unbounded plunder, expansionism and appropriation). Common schooling should inspire healthy citizenship as a non-extremist love of country, a mind to see it clearly and a reach to make it better; and an open mind to value others.

Separatist institutions fragment and divide, and politicians and public officials should avoid pandering to separatist academies, regardless of their names or underwriters. The US president is wrong to propose funding of charters instead of directing his administration to work diligently to improve the important tradition and process of public schooling. The public treasury should promote and enhance public schools and improve professionalism, teaching and learning, and the content and materials that support these. Common schooling serves the common good. The notion of public/private partnership is a nonentity, a ruse, a trick, a maneuver; public is not private, and *partner* implies what isn't: a match of equals. The mission and goals of the two arenas, private profit and public good, are separate and distinct and should not be conjoined or given the pretense of conjoining.

Public Is Public, Private Is Private

Pandering pacifies with contempt. Pandering, for example, to a sect, identity, or tribe; pandering to momentary hysteria brought on by self-loathing or dissatisfaction with place, position, or performance pacifies for momentary gain and prevents anything good to rise in its wake. Pandering to religion and religionists; pandering to ideology, to left, right, or center fanatics; pandering to a singular view or to personal prejudices; pandering to blue state or red state, to southern states or eastern states, to one country against another; pandering (prostituting or pimping) for oil or sex or money or weapons sales; pandering or extreme partisanship creates chaos, endless conflict, loss of trust, dangerous ignorance, and deterioration of the health of peoples and the planet. In the game of pandering politics, nothing is sacrosanct except the return on an unprincipled investment.

There should be a distinct line drawn between what is a public matter and what are purely private matters.

Matters of reproduction, religion, and sexuality are private and should not be funded or regulated by governmental systems or catered to one way or another by elected officials—except where crimes are being committed, such as people and institution's sexual abuse of children or sexual assault on campus or in militaries. If someone wants to change his or her sex or sexuality, the government should not interfere or pay for such changes. If private foundations or churches wish to engage in charity, let them fund such practices with their own legacy funds or privately raised funds, not channeled through or siphoned off the public treasure. Public is public. Private is private.

Public matters are what provide for the common good and public welfare: disease prevention, scientific research, and education on disease cures. We must remember that private interests distributed and government officials allowed cancer-causing cigarettes on college campuses, just as killing programs are insinuated into college curricula today. Negligence, carelessness, failure of oversight, failure of regulation and regular monitoring of regulatory laws ensure public harm in perpetuity— mind and body diseased for private profit. Let private companies and institutions peddle their goods and try to persuade others to buy, but let the public institutions teach skills of and propensity for discernment, critical judgment in order to decide whether to be convinced and whether or not to buy products or services. It should be the mission of public entities, processes such as schooling, and institutions of learning to instill skills of discernment and critical judgment beneficial to health. The purpose of the public sector should be to enable the public to subsist in good mental, physical, psychological, and social health. The public sector—government of, by, and for the people—should be the source of the public's defense against the excesses of private interests.

Panderers and other self-interested people have blurred the line between private and public, to the point that it is almost entirely erased; this breach has caused a wider gulf between and among people. Public officials who cater to and shift between one sector and another or hop from one frill or fad to another, as suits their reelection fancy or hold on power, do great harm to the country. They sacrifice essential institutions that would, in the words of the US Constitution, promote the general welfare and provide for the common defense.

True Basics Take Priority

Basic rights enshrined in the *Universal Declaration of Human Rights* should not be meted out expediently or based on class and other superficialities or held hostage to bribery or affluence. Human rights are not luxuries but are matters of health and proper functioning of individuals, together with the health and proper functioning of society at large. Therefore, the priorities of government proffered by its officials should be based on these basic, objectively predetermined principles.

Basic rights include shelter, not a mortgage or gated community or some nonsensical "American dream." No one should languish under bridges, on sidewalks, or in tunnels. Such places do not constitute human shelters but shelters for vermin, rats, and roaches. Provisions should be made for permanent livable shelter with assistance to rise into self-sufficiency. This is not Communism or socialism or the condescension of obliged charity. It is humanity, humankind, relating with humanity.

Basic rights should include equal access and opportunity for people of varieties of difference, such as gender and sexual orientation, but not public funding of "emotional" pets, sex change, or psychoanalysis pertaining to any of these.

Basic rights should promote public health, not panderers, and exclude gamers, such as narcotics growers and those who push narcotics, including manufacturers, street sellers, and physician sellers. "Cadillac Medicare" claims for activities and procedures such as cosmetic surgery, fitness training, athletic club memberships, or pets for subjectively determined emotional conditions do not fall within the content or intent of basic or universal human rights.

Basics rights do not extend to "dreams" or other propagandized, advertised, or delusional entrapments. Those who "dream" are usually asleep or sleepwalking, and until brainwashed into believing otherwise, even a child knows this simple truth.

The basic right of all nations is peace and sovereignty. War breaches the peace of nations, even when wrapped in a cloak of humanitarian aid. Violent aggression is never humanitarian. Those who plead to sit as equals, and do so with honor, around conference tables, discussing and resolving conflicts and ending wars, are the true champions of human rights. Nobody is out to get us or our stuff or our values, and the claim of terrorists, enemies, or axis of evil is usually a creation of panderers with narrow minds and private agendas, intent on cementing their own power by instilling fear and driving dissention and division among the masses and various groups of people.

Priorities set by the government and its people should not be pandered priorities—anything for anyone who pays the most or makes the loudest noise or threatens to divide political parties or refuses to build a plant in City X or Y. The deepest pockets, those brazen enough to commit bribery, should not be priority setters. The *normalization* of entrenched corruption that pervades public office, up and down the governmental spectrum, is anything but normal. Yet how many times have we wept at this sad ring of truth? In the presidential campaign season leading toward the 2016 election, there was a clear call "for meaningful policies that would help average Americans," policies concerning healthcare, wages, infrastructure, and the end of US foreign wars. But, Natylie Baldwin wrote, neither "mainstream Democrats" nor "Republicans" will deliver on America's basic needs "because"— though they will not admit this to the American people — "their donors don't want them to." Natylie Baldwin is co-author of *Ukraine: Zbig's Grand Chessboard & How the West Was Checkmated*. Her article appears online in a March 15, 2018, post at *Consortium News*.

Priorities with a view toward future generations should be set by the people and public office with the aim of lifting and improving the lives of people, the quality of life, public institutions, and society. This means that education, learning, creation—not war-making and arms-selling, not killing and training for killing—should be the priorities of a nation aspiring to be great *and good*.

Priorities of a good nation build instead of destroying. Greatness is not measured in terms of numbers killed and maimed, cultures destroyed, nations and regions thrown into chaos, peoples warring against one another, numbers of states failed, or terrorists created. A great nation is measured in terms of the principles it practices and the priorities it chooses: the building and sustaining of healthy relations among peoples and nations at home and abroad.

Pandering Partnered with Propaganda, Fear, Violence

Why build a wall if not out of fear?
—Hon. Vicente Fox
Former president of Mexico

PANDERERS WRAP FEAR in pretty ribbons of false patriotism injected continuously like a drug, numbing the people (the body politic, the population) to the sinister priorities of partnered profit-taking and the raging of endless conflict and aggression.

US Leadership: Mexico

In a 2017 speech at Case Western Reserve University in Ohio, the former president of Mexico said, "Fear is not a good advisor."

Vicente Fox said that while he does not support open borders and he understands the right of sovereignty of all nations, including the United States, he recognizes also that the two North American neighbors, Mexico and the United States, have a shared history, shared issues, and shared responsibility. In the current era, he said, "The relationship between Mexico and the United States has never been more crucial." Our "shared border means we must act together to solve mutual problems and strengthen beneficial ties. . . . Immigration reform is a piece of that process . . . which would include a permanent path to citizenship for millions of Latinos now living in the United States." Looking toward the future, Fox said, "Bilateral input is critical in creating the most effective immigration policy." His advice to US congressional and executive leadership was to "respond to the challenge with a sound, intelligent and common-sense plan. Make immigration an asset to both countries."

In an earlier opinion piece, Fox had also addressed the immigration issue. In the broadest sense, he wrote, "Migration is an advantage in a global economy." Immigrants "contribute to economic development in the countries where they work." They provide "critical skill sets and services," and "Mexican immigrants are often heroic. They take big risks in hopes of creating better lives for themselves and their families. They are immensely hardworking and ambitious."

The United States in particular "should value the contributions of Latin American immigrants as a new chapter in the great American story." As a practical matter, "migration is a two-way street." As there are Mexican immigrants in the United States, there are also many US citizens who call Mexico home. Regardless of where they originate or where they migrate to, human beings want respect and are deserving of "respect, freedom, and opportunity for a better life." In a sense of humanity to be admired and taken as an example, Fox concludes, "We need to build bridges that foster migration. Not walls at the border."

US Leadership: Russia

In the period leading up to the 2016 US presidential election, after the results were in and the new president seated, the drumbeat of "the Russians are coming" persisted, as in a chamber of echoes. One after another writer decried the madness, the slough, the hostility of partisan cronies and an opinionated, unprofessional news press. Their propagandized mantra devoid of hard evidence, "the Russians did it," was swallowed whole by an undiscerning public.

In the heat of unending hysteria and the back-and-forth attack and counterattack in the preelection results period, Patrick Henningsen asked some deeply disturbing questions that Americans should consider, not as partisans but as citizens:

> Are American politicians so callous as to tempt geopolitical conflict in order to further their short-term political ambitions?

And

> Has American political life . . . arrived at such a dark cul-
> de-sac [bottom of the bag] where politicians in power [he
> notes that Hillary Rodham Clinton's wild hyperbolic rants
> about the Kremlin and WikiLeaks were backed up by US
> President Barack Obama] are so insecure as to make up and
> propagate wild international conspiracy theories—in the
> middle a national election cycle?

In his post–Election Day analysis, Henningsen observed that many mainstream writers were so deeply submerged in Western-generated American or British propaganda that they apparently missed or were "completely oblivious" to hard evidence-based news: that former US secretary of state John Kerry "had been caught lying to the world at the UN about what Russia supposedly did in the Ukraine, Crimea, and Syria," that former UN ambassador Samantha Power's shrill antics at the UN had been "an embarrassment" to the United States before "a world audience," that US admiral John Kirby had come undone when unable to "defend his own lies . . . during a U.S. State Department press briefing."

The loss of US government and Western media credibility rang round the world in the Obama years. Particularly "on Syria," Henningsen said. US politicians "lied so much and so often that most serious people around the world" stopped believing anything that came out of the Barack Obama administration. In Western media, confirmation bias was both chronic and systemic; so much so that American and European bloggers "disgusted with their government's duplicity and poor conduct in world affairs and international relations" (e.g., against Russia, Syria, Yemen, and others) had "every right and responsibility to set the record straight."

But the unfounded "Russians are coming," Russia-Putin hacking, Trump-Russian "collusion" drums of hostiles were unrelenting. Veteran investigative reporter Robert Parry, whose experience extends to establishment media and reporting during the Iran-Contra era, observed the irony that the hearsay material had originated from and was purchased and peddled to the US press not by the Donald Trump presidential campaign but by the Hillary Rodham Clinton presidential campaign. Nevertheless, without proof, journalists joined the "Russians stole our elections" hysteria. "There is no professional justification for journalists joining in a TV-and-print lynch mob," Robert Parry wrote. Clear-thinking Americans and others mindful of history will remember "where such wrongheadedness leads"—in recent times, "to [WMD] groupthink" that caused another series of years of violent aggression against Iraq (US torment of Iraq's people extends further back, to the late twentieth century's Gulf War, 1990–1995), the assassination of its head of state, the endless conflict and suffering of its people, and in earlier times, US Senator Joe McCarthy's McCarthyism, which destroyed American lives and livelihoods under spurious charges of having been "unpatriotic" for holding differing thoughts. As Barry puts it, the targeted people were "smeared as unpatriotic" because of "dissident political views." (Interestingly, or not, Joseph Raymond "Joe" McCarthy and Hillary Diane Rodham rose from insulated rural and small suburban-city environments in bordering US Midwestern states.)

Small minds, self-serving politicians, misplaced power, and its reckless abuse took upon themselves the combined plan of bringing a US head of state, demonizing a foreign superpower, and risking nuclear war. Parry wrote "even Donald Trump" does not deserve "to be railroaded" or "run out of town on a rail," using "any pretext" and risking annihilation, "escalating the risks of a nuclear war with Russia."

[Deceased during the course of work on my manuscript, writer and Consortium News editor Robert Parry (June 24, 1949 – January 27, 2018) was an American investigative journalist best known for his role in covering the Iran-Contra affair for the Associated Press (AP) and *Newsweek*. In later years, he was the founder of the Consortium for Independent Journalism Inc (CIJ), a non-profit US-based independent news service that publishes the website Consortium News.]

US Leadership: Muslims

In his turn at the helm, the new US president proposed a US entry ban on Muslims or people originating from Muslim countries, notably countries against which the US is either at war, is funding aggression, or is otherwise aiding and abetting conflict. A refrain of violence answers the call of violence, as in chorale-style call-and-response—but with unmusical deadliness! Islamophobia emboldened by rhetoric of the hate "becomes a socially acceptable form of bigotry" manifesting ultimately "in discrimination" and "even violence," writes attorney and law professor Faisal Kutty.

While it is perhaps unwise or impossible to find a straight line between the new US president's executive order banning Muslim travel into the United States and the Sunday rampage at the Centre Culturel Islamique de Québec that left six dead and nineteen others wounded, Canadian broadcaster Michael Enright essayed in the CBC *Sunday Edition* program of February 3, 2017,

> We should not be surprised that fear can be stoked. Anger can migrate. Vulnerability and innocence can be exploited in a world going mad.

President Donald Trump's "travel ban and anticipated Muslim registry did not rise out of thin air" but finds root "in the *culture of fear* [emphasis added] and targeting of Muslims nurtured by too many in positions of power on both sides of the [US/Canada] border since the early 1990s" and "most aggressively since [September 11, 2001] and 'The War on Terror.'" (Professor Kutty was writing for the *Toronto Star* on February 1, 2017.)

The "legacy of 'othering' and dehumanization prepped the populace," and Donald J. Trump tapped into it. It reached a "watershed moment" in the twenty-teens, but in Western politics and popular culture, the demonization of Muslims has a long history. In relatively recent times, from "a well-funded network of professional merchants of hate on the fringe" to a "small segment" of US and Canadian political partisans, the anti-Muslim fervor has "reached heights never before imagined by most analysts."

Words have consequences, often in violence, as violence has consequences in violence. "Political rhetoric and online hate groups cross-pollinate. . . . 'It is an ecosystem.'" Though politicians use words differently—*some more, some less crudely*, some in ordinary tones, some in the nuanced tones of an orator—"they all swim in the same pool," said Ryerson University professor Kamal Al-Solaylee (quoted in a *Los Angeles Times* article by Alyssa Favreau). Canada, he said, "is a great country [and] there is a sense that we're better than the United States," but in both countries, "words and rhetoric and this fever pitch discourse [against Muslims] will have consequences on people's lives."

Faced with the smoldering embers of massacre, they cue each other and chant together: "we are shocked," "our thoughts and prayers are with you." But the dead hear no words of solace or politicians' pageantry of mourning, Enright concluded the Sunday morning after. The facts remain indisputable.

In one case, human beings targeted human beings "in the literal sight of a gun." In the other, human beings targeted human beings "with the flourish of a presidential pen." And a vast majority of populations shrug in actual or feigned ignorance.

Sowing Ignorance

What happens when large numbers of people pander, peddle and profit from propaganda; when people are deliberately bamboozled; when people aspire to and benefit from what the peddlers peddle and the profiteers profit from? It is what happens when values are distorted or reduced to materialism, as implied in simplistic notions like the American Dream and bucket lists (notions as ridiculous as fielding the "bucket list lady" as a candidate for the US presidency). What happens when the masses are poorly educated, undereducated, untrained or poorly trained, and/or miseducated? What happens when seemingly intelligent people ignore and fail to take responsibility for a deeply troubled USA, in a world where millions of people suffer terribly and endlessly? What happens when, for a long time, flagrantly flawed policies and practices of depraved power, public officials and power brokers have normalized violence, corruption, negligence, sheer carelessness, and indifference resulting in deep and unrelenting discontent within populations domestic and global? One contributing outlet calling itself progressive media or programs for peace airs what it terms "neo-Nazism" absent critical context. Context is essential in good journalism. But little of what is aired nowadays is either good or journalism. Most of it is some person, partisan or group's narrowly drawn or uninformed opinion.

The *Democracy Now!* headlines on November 22, 2017, rebroadcasted without historical context or cultural comparisons an excerpt from Richard Spencer's pitiable outburst:

> Heil Trump! Heil our people! Heil victory! To be white is to be a striver, a crusader, an explorer and a conqueror. We build. We produce. We go upward. And we recognize the central lie of American race relations. We don't exploit other groups. We—we don't gain anything from their presence. They need us, and not the other way around. America was, until this past generation, a white country, designed

for ourselves and our posterity. It is our creation, it is our inheritance, and it belongs to us.

The *Democracy Now!* selective screed falls far short of a smidgen of the whole story. Further research finds that Richard Bertrand Spencer, described as "an American white nationalist," was in 2014 "deported from Budapest, Hungary, and via the Schengen Agreement, is banned from 26 countries in Europe for three years" for having tried "to organize a National Policy Institute Conference, a conference for white nationalists."

In the United States, Spencer reportedly resides in one or more places: Whitefish, Montana (located on the western side of the continental divide, near Glacier National Park, home to a ski resort on Big Mountain called Whitefish Mountain Resort; 2010 census demographics showing 95.8% white, 0.5% African American, 0.8% Native American, 0.8% Asian, 0.1% Pacific Islander, 0.3% from other races, and 1.7% from two or more races. Hispanic or Latino of any race made up 2.8% of the population); and/or Arlington, Virginia (Northern Virginia, the second-largest principal city of the Washington, DC Metropolitan, in 2000; 28% of its residents foreign-born: 63.8% non-Hispanic white, 8.9% non-Hispanic black or African American, 0.8% non-Hispanic Native American, 9.9% non-Hispanic Asian [2.0% Indian, 1.7% Chinese, 1.1% Filipino, 0.9% Korean, 0.7% Vietnamese, 2.7% other Asian], 0.1% Pacific Islander, 0.29% non-Hispanic other races, 3.0% non-Hispanics reporting two or more races, 15.4% of the population was Hispanic or Latino of any race [3.4% Salvadoran, 2.0% Bolivian, 1.7% Mexican, 1.5% Guatemalan, 0.8% Puerto Rican, 0.7% Peruvian, 0.6% Colombian]). Richard Bertrand Spencer was apparently married and separated from a native Russian.

This narrow brand of *Democracy Now!* and other lazy reporting is like limiting slavery to the United States or to the US South or like saying only white people are racialists, chauvinists, sexists, or bigots. A narrow brand of reporting gives a reporter's or news outlet's point of view but neither truth nor even objective reporting.

Moreover, narrow or lazy reporting, in its intent on a slant or point of view, fails to present prior conditions or underlying causes that enter into and are essential to understanding a particular event. Large numbers of America's youth are, not unlike refugees in foreign lands, discarded, thrown to the winds where predators prey. Many are reduced to stealing and offering sex for food. Rigorously documented studies have shown in recent years that in this land where some are free, "significant numbers of teenagers" are reduced to stealing, dealing drugs, being exploited sexually, and committing themselves to jails in order to eat and/or to "put food on the table for themselves and their families."

As the Obama double terms were ending, Kate Randall reported that the "catastrophic state of social life in the United States" is the result of "decades of social counter-revolution carried out by" the two tyrannical political parties. The William Jefferson "Bill" Clinton regime gutted the US welfare system without corresponding jobs programs, thus ensuring "a vast increase in poverty and hunger." Radicalism sometimes rises when one person or group in desperate need senses that the others are getting what he, she or they also deserve and need; and politicians' priorities drive an ever-widening wedge between the desperate of both camps.

The Obama regime ramped up militarism instead of attending to the basic needs of America's people. Billions—$8.6 billion—were cut from the "the Supplemental Nutritional Assistance Program (SNAP), the food stamp program." Successive administrations' "destructive negligence and impossible requirements in an increasingly sluggish employment market, globalization and offshoring, inferior education systems for the masses, and relatively few unskilled and living-wage jobs set the stage for hundreds of thousands to lose their benefits before the end of 2016." Joblessness and an absence of essentials create a void in search of meaning in one's life.

The ordinary Joe or Jasmine viewing the forty-fourth president and his entourage came away with the impression that Mr. President and company were living in a distant galaxy far removed from ordinary people. Instead of providing for the general welfare, pandering politicians were slashing social programs and denying the common good and a good society to fund violent aggression at home and abroad. This trend continued under the forty-fifth US president.

The two reports Randall references, she says, "cast a sharp light on the social catastrophe in the United States and its impact on America's youth." Not unlike people caught in US wars abroad or displaced by war and conflict and deserted in refugee camps for an eternity, the United States of America has many vulnerable young people: "food-insecure teens—girls in particular—vulnerable to . . . sexual exploitation." Randall reports that teens canvassed in all locations covered by the studies "spoke of girls having sex for money to pay for food and other needs," often "'transactional dating' in which the teen regularly sees and has sex with someone, usually an older man, in exchange for food, meals, cash or other material goods."

This unspeakable condition of children lacks the sex appeal so loved by major print and broadcast media as shown by their round the clock embrace of the relatively recent celebrity "Me toos." Somehow these deep concerns for the young, *who are the future*, are just not headline hysterical or salacious enough to attract *Democracy Now!*, CNN, NPR, pandering politicians, or more "Me too" celebrities.

Failing institutions of the press and public education are failing Americans. Brazilian philosopher, educator, author, and scholar Paulo Reglus Neves Freire (September 19, 1921–May 2, 1997) counseled on the importance of a good education, as did US presidents Madison and Lincoln. Through the process of learning, pupils "can make and remake themselves," Freire said. They are enabled "to take responsibility for themselves as beings capable of knowing— of knowing that they know and knowing that they do not know." Today in the United States, the institution and processes of education have become so politicized—trapped in one or another tribal identity or ideology and/or the cult of profiteering greed—that it no longer deserves the name "education."

The head of the US Department of Education under the relatively new administration in Federal Washington (2017–) is a political fundraising relative of Amway billionaires and military mercenaries whose only connections with US education are her religious school baccalaureate degree in economics and a preference for and promotion of profit-driven privatized US education. Commenting on the new regime, Esther Galen wrote in March of 2017 that "billionaires and their foundations see opportunities to increase their wealth through school privatization." These men and women are astute in "setting up charter schools, many of which accept vouchers," reaching back to the Bill Clinton 1990s initiative of New Markets Tax Credit that "combines 'the private sector and the federal government—to bring economic and community development to low-income communities.'" The "race to the top" upside-down policy of the Obama government saw a proliferation of charter schools and "edubusinesses in Michigan, the home state of now– US secretary of education, Betsy DeVos. In Detroit, Michigan, "the DeVos family's policies" have reportedly "resulted in a battery of pro-privatization legislation and the control of 80 percent of charters by for-profit businesses."

In this noneducational, profit-taking proposition, "the capitalist market" is the determinant of "how and whether" school-age youngsters receive an education. "Parents, as 'consumers,'" Esther Galen writes, "will have a choice as to where they send their children to be educated and evaluate what they bought. If they're not happy with the school giving the education they purchased, they can look for another one, *as though they were buying a pair of shoes*" (emphasis added).

Hitches abound in this profiteering anti-education scheme. One is the fact that not all parents are able to make informed choices (that's one of the reasons the common school was a great idea and has worked but has been allowed to decline). Another hitch is, the wealthier the education consumer, the better the chances for his or her school-age youngster attending a good school and receiving a quality education. Working classes; poor people; and second-language, illiterate, or poorly literate parents need not apply. Another hitch is, since not all students are equally prepared, academically, for certain grade-level entries, those pupils not performing or conforming to profiteers' bottom line are subject to discrimination, dismissal, and denial. "While private schools choose" which students to admit and retain, "public schools are legally bound to serve all children, including special education, English as a Second Language (ESL) and low-income students," Galen writes. The voucher scheme robs public schools of "desperately needed resources" to pay for "private and parochial schools."

In the realm of US education, sadly, is another example of the destructive nature and consequences of pandering politics. The rich aided and abetted by pandering politicians' policies further enrich themselves, while everybody else—the majority of families and school-age young people—is abandoned to chart their course to privatized prisons, drug markets or separatist clans, death or injury in war or on neighborhood streets, or further economic disadvantage. Denied proper development through quality education and training, the young are effectively caged, stunted in growth, and vulnerable to manipulation by external sources in "the underworld" or "counterculture," in mass media, or from the actions and rhetoric of government officials. The loss of the young is a critical loss to society. Their impairment impairs society.

> We must build a new country that belongs to all of us, a country where no one ever has to feel like [an *untouchable*] no one cares about.

> [Perhaps an] answer lies [in seeing] that our poor neighbors, who may be different than us, are [also] struggling. (Writer and playwright Jonna Ivin)

III

Values: Priorities of Violence or Nonviolence

We as a nation have opted to be ruler of the world and all that we survey. And however benevolent and kind we might wish to be, the violence that surrounds us in our streets and in our homes and in our world is evidence that we have succumbed to the temptation of the desert. We face a deep and profound spiritual crisis.

—Rev. Dr. Joan B. Campbell
(Riverside Church, New York City, April 21, 1991)

MORALLY AND ETHICALLY principled leadership has been hard to come by for a long time. Americans are led to believe that up is down, wrong is right, violence is peace. We accept priorities dripping in blood, boasting American values without connecting the two as one.

Priorities set by leadership and issued through policies at home and abroad are the windows through which the world views our values—values that declare who we really are, who America really is and what it stands for, and what standards characterize America's leadership. There is no getting around it. The act is the indisputable evidence: We *are* what we do. And our values today can be reduced to a single word—*violence*.

US Foreign Aggression

Despite unspeakable suffering at home and abroad, US war-making marches on, and one after another US president pledges his allegiance to endless war.

In a news article on February 3, 2015, Andre Damon observed accurately that the two major US political parties are virtually identical in their values. They represent, Damon said, "different factions of the same ruling oligarchy and pursue a common agenda of austerity, militarism and the build-up of the repressive powers of the state." Violence!

The Obama government's budget proposal in 2015 increased "Pentagon (War Department) spending by seven percent" with "an additional $38 billion" that brought "the total defense budget to $534 billion" and was coupled with a separate funding package of $51 billion for the war on Syria together with the then–twelve-year-old war against Iraq and the fourteen-year-old war against Afghanistan. Wars cause more wars in an endless cycle of violence. Twenty-five years (1991–2016) of unending wars led by Republican and Democratic party presidents and fifteen years of the War on Terror have caused the deaths and suffering of millions and have led to bitter conflicts and recriminations over US policy and demands for major escalations in military violence. In 2018 the US will have been engaged in violent aggression against the Iraqi people for fifteen years, fifteen years, that is, since the 2003 US-led war against the sovereign nation of Iraq. It was a war, Chris Marsden recalled in a March 17, 2018, article, "based on a torrent of lies." The US and UK "manufactured intelligence" to justify the war; and when their inspectors "found no evidence" to support their claim of Iraq's "nuclear or chemical weapons program," the US secretary of state, Colin Powell, went to the United Nations and presented a "wholly manufactured slide show, purporting to show photographic 'evidence' of Iraq hiding unconventional weapons." A month later, on March 20, 2003, the US began bombing the people of this nation. And US officials continue to call for aggression not only against the sovereign state of Syria but against the whole of the Middle East and farther north and east into the Russian Federation and the People's Republic of China.

On the road to the White House, the man who became the forty-fifth US president seemed to have promised to mend foreign relations and rebuild domestic structures, but as in earlier performances by campaigning political candidates, the words proved empty. In 2017, the new president signed a $700 billion increase in military spending and the operational capabilities defense budget. That summer, the US House of Representatives also presented the new president with multimillion dollar reductions in funding for the US Department of (Public) Education, Health and Human Services, Substance Abuse and Mental Health, the Centers for Disease Control, and Health

Resources and Services Administration (Fiscal Year 2018 Labor, Health and Human Services, and Education draft funding bill). In his first State of the Union message in late January 2017, the president promised to build up the nation's weapons of mass destruction.

Together with public officials' setting of policies and priorities of violence are religious establishments, mass media, and various for-profit and purportedly not-for-profit groups' enthusiastic approvals of and excuses for US foreign affairs violence. A US president is embraced as presidential, and women are applauded as strong when they threaten other nations and bomb foreign villages. The new president promised peace and then performed a State of the Union speech resurrecting the old "axis of evil" mantra, reciting the same old canard: the world is against us, challenging "our interests, our economy, and our values."

US leaders tell the world we "value life" while taking the lives of peoples across the world. Those who survive see the contradiction between words and action: America really values killing, slaughter, destruction, the suffering of others, and the ultimate annihilation of America itself.

Western values, as of Iraqi children, are killing and maiming the children of Yemen. A 2017 report found that Yemen's children, caught in war and conflict, are forced into homelessness "with limited access to food, basic healthcare or clean water [1.8 million children facing acute malnutrition]." Significant numbers of Yemen's "396,086 suspected cholera cases" are children. The young are "torn from their schools and forced to live in makeshift camps" and are "headed toward a future marked by fear and uncertainty" (2017 OCHA report).

The young are young but not blind or deaf. Americans are impressionable. And unlike wealth and prosperity, their country's leadership character and celebration of easy violence trickles down to ordinary people. During the political campaigns leading into 2016, one of America's female senior citizens who disliked one of the candidates said to me she would pay to have the candidate she opposed killed. She would not do it herself, she said, but she would contribute to the funding of the kill. The valuing of violence by Americans cuts across the political spectrum and sectarian affiliations.

We tear nations apart. We build no livable shelters for refugees or for the homeless or stateless. We aid no lasting peace, mend no relations, and ensure no self-determination. We stand and watch—perhaps unintentionally aiding and abetting—as America itself comes undone. We are our own true enemy.

Former US congressman Ron Paul was well aware of the America's cognitive dissonance, its conflict between words and deeds, between pretexts and reality. "There is a lot of foreign anger directed toward us [US leadership and so Americans]," the lawmaker said.

> [But] Americans do not lie awake at night fearing that someone from Afghanistan will come and kill them. This has not happened, it is not happening, and it will not happen.

Yet this relatively new US president, Donald John Trump, in lockstep with his predecessors, believes that, in Paul's words, "we should be killing more people in Afghanistan."

US Foreign War on Press Freedom

As with their claim of valuing life, Americans pretend to value freedom of expression and a free press, but only as it suits their whims or pandering politics.

A case in point—together with a generalized hostility toward Russians and their government—is US lawmakers' attack on international press outlets Sputnik and RT (Russia Today). In an atmosphere of hysterical whatever was done Russia did it, the US Congress decided to essentially ban these news organizations. The lawmakers drafted legislation labeling them as foreign agents representing foreign powers subject to US infiltration, an out-and-out breach of international and US domestic laws of free press. The US "free" press met this aggression with silence signaling assent.

I listen regularly to online news and programming by RT and Sputnik, and I know them to be, as advertised, legitimate broadcasting outlets that provide highly informative news and commentary, superior programming with consistently highly professional journalists and interviewers. Their work is equal to, often better than, and certainly a viable alternative to Britain's BBC and Germany's Deutsche Welle, the latter two enthusiastically accepted by United States officials. For its part, news and programming that are purely US produced and broadcast or published, with few exceptions, is riddled with opinion, biased pseudo-experts, propaganda, anonymous sources, and sensationalism sandwiched between mind-numbing drug and car commercials.

Nevertheless, the Russian press does not measure up to the US standard of what a free press should be, so in 2017, the US Justice Department threatened RT America with expulsion if the organization did not "register as a foreign agent" (which it was not) engaged in "disseminating propaganda" (which it was not doing).

Reaching back to the early twentieth century, US lawmakers dredged up something called the Foreign Agents Registration Act of 1938 then added to the earlier act with the Agents Registration Modernization and Enforcement Act and slapped them against RT. Having been cast as a "foreign agent" representing "the interest of foreign powers," RT, a news organization, would be required to disclose their foreign relationship and provide "information about related activities and finances." This is, in fact, violence against (aggression, assault on) press freedom, which a truly great nation, a strong nation—confident in itself—would have no need of. One wonders if US officials and those they pander to have another agenda—that of cutting competition with their inferior product of round-the-clock propagandized and commercialized news and information or infomercial banality.

As with many acts of pandering public figures and officeholders, these actions are destructive of essential institutions (not to mention an abuse of power) and ideals (values) Americans claim to uphold and indeed hold up and "export" to other peoples and nations. The Congress of the United States, without care of consequences, uses "any methods to achieve its goals," Andrei Akulov responded, "including trampling on core 'American values' such as freedom of speech.... The hunchback does not see his own hump."

US government officials' silencing of alternative news and views, even more than the breach of international convention and US domestic law, amounts to an act of tyranny, as observed by America's fourth president and the father of the US Constitution: "If tyranny and oppression come to this land," Madison said, "it will be in the guise of fighting a foreign enemy." We are our enemy.

Neglect: Priorities, Poverty, Loss of Faith

Although the United States ranks among the world's richest and most powerful and technologically innovative countries, "neither its wealth nor its power nor its technology is being harnessed to address the situation in which 40 million people" languish in poverty.

Child poverty rates in the United States "are the highest amongst the six richest countries—Canada, the United Kingdom, Ireland, Sweden and Norway" (OCHR, United Nations Office of the High Commissioner for Human Rights). Among America's youth, the rate of poverty "is the highest across the OECD," with one quarter of US youth subsisting "in poverty compared to less than 14% across OECD [Organization for Economic Cooperation and Development]" countries.

In its 2017 report, "State of the Union Poverty," the Stanford Center on Poverty and Inequality found that poverty persists in one in four Negro (*my interntional historic usage, no offense intended*) and Native Americans, one in five Latino Americans, and one in ten Asian and Caucasian Americans. While the poverty rate for Caucasians appears comparatively low, as this group makes up the majority of the US population, it comprises the majority of the nation's poor. The 25 percent of US household heads (Negro and Latino Americans) "account for 44 percent of the nation's poor."

Poverty rates persist geographically in US cities, regionally in the US South, and in deep concentrations among Negroes (33%) and Latinos (28%) in the rural South; Negroes in the rural Northeast (31%), and American Indians in the rural West (32%). The researchers concluded that the United States remains a deeply divided nation of at least "two Americas."

The United States ranks thirty-sixth in the world for providing and ensuring "access to water and sanitation" and carries the world's highest incarceration rate—more than Turkmenistan, El Salvador, Cuba, Thailand, and the Russian Federation. The rate of imprisonment in the United States is "nearly 5 times the OECD average."

Callous policy proposals, extending back at least to the William Jefferson Clinton era, to push people off welfare into work (not unlike the trend of privatized hospitals pushing patients unable to pay on to the streets) presume erroneously "that there are a great many jobs out there waiting to be filled by individuals with low educational standards," people "often suffering disabilities of one kind or another, sometimes burdened with a criminal record (perhaps for the crime of homelessness or not being able to pay a traffic ticket), and with no training or meaningful assistance to obtain employment." Thus, for these people, there is no access to work, let alone meaningful work at living wages. For example, the researchers spoke with big box store workers "who could not survive on a full-time wage" with these companies "without also relying on food stamps." An estimated "$6 billion dollars go from the SNAP program [Supplemental Nutrition Assistance Program] to support such workers, thus providing a huge virtual subsidy to the relevant corporations." Yet government leaders prefer demonizing and disparaging to fixing conditions and solving domestic problems.

While US leaders constantly attack Asian nations and project the United States as an exceptional nation, American students demonstrate glaringly inferior learning in the basics (mathematics, reading, science), with some American students allowed to proudly opt out of taking exams. On a 2015 international assessment, the Program for International Student Assessment (PISA), the US reportedly ranked thirty-fifth (having dropped from twenty-eighth in 2012) in math among seventy-two countries, an estimated 540,000 students, and remained unchanged in reading and science rankings. The executive chairman of America Achieves told the press that the United States needs "to make dramatic progress in showing educational improvement for students." Leading the rankings on the three basics were Asian countries, and topping the lot in all subjects was the Southeast Asian nation of Singapore, a diverse population on the Malay Peninsula near the South China Sea that demonstrates true values supporting a rewarding quality of life, i.e., education and health and welfare of its people.US government leaders' breach of basic human rights (health, education, housing, work) standards has wide-ranging consequences, not least of which is the loss of faith in government that manifests itself in apathy; withdrawal from society; a lack of care for life itself; violence, often out of frustration and a lack of meaning in life; and often the refusal to exert minimal effort in carrying out minor citizenry duties. A 2012 Quartz article reported data showing that voter turnout in fifty-eight countries exceeded US voter turnout. Countries such as Iran (also Nicaragua and Ukraine)—often publicly demonized, slandered and ridiculed by US leaders and media—take their civic duty considerably more seriously than does the United States of America. The portrait of voter turnout:

Uruguay (96.1% in 2009), •Ecuador (90.8% in 2009), •Uzbekistan (89.8% in 2007), •Rwanda (89.2% in 2010), •Angola (87.5% in 1992), •Turkmenistan (87.0% in 2012), •Peru (86.2% in 2011). •Bolivia (85.6% in 2009), •Tunisia (85.2% in 2009), •Equatorial Guinea (83.0% in 2009), •Belarus (81.7% in 2010), •Tajikistan (80.8% in 2006), •Venezuela (78.9% in 2012), •Cyprus (78.8% in 2008), •Argentina (77.4% in 2011), •Brazil (77.3% in 2010), •Armenia (77.2% in 2008), •East Timor (76.3% in 2012),

•Iran (75.5% in 2009), •Philippines (75.1% in 2004), •Indonesia (74.8% in 2004), •Taiwan (74.3% in 2012), •Malawi (73.9% in 2009), •Gambia (73.5% in 2011), •Kazakhstan (72.7% in 2011), •Congo-Brazzaville (72.6% in 2009), •El Salvador (72.4% in 2009), •Nicaragua (71.8% in 2011), •Sao Tome and Principe (71.3% in 2011), •France (71.2% in 2012), •Sri Lanka (70.9% in 2010), •Dominican Republic (70.2% in 2012), Ghana (69.8% in 2008), •Maldives (69.3% in 2008), •Panama (69.0% in 2009), •Iceland (68.9% in 2012), •Benin (68.4% in 2011), •Ukraine (67.9% in 2010), •Namibia (67.6% in 2009), •Palau (67.6% in 2008), •Finland (67.5% in 2012), •Azerbaijan (66.9% in 2008), •Algeria (65.9% in 2009), •Croatia (65.2% in 2010), •Mexico (64.6% in 2012), •Republic of Korea (64.2% in 2007), •Montenegro (63.5% in 2008), •Russia (63.4% in 2012), •Costa Rica (62.3% in 2010), •Sierra Leone (62.0% in 2007), •Guatemala (61.4% in 2011), •Togo (61.3% in 2010), •Slovenia (61.3% in 2007), •Romania (59.2% in 2009), •Chile (59.1% in 2010), •Bosnia and Herzegovina (58.8% in 2010), •Burundi (58.7% in 2010), •Chad (57.9% in 2011), •USA (57.5% of voting-age Americans cast ballots in the presidential election in 2008).

In the 2016 US presidential election, an estimated 55.7 percent of "the US voting-age population cast ballots" (US Census Bureau figures), a percentage that is "well below turnout levels typical in most other developed 'democracies.'" Drew DeSilver was reporting for the Pew Research organization in May 15, 2017, post. The voter turnout figure put the United States behind most member states of the Organization for Economic Cooperation and Development. Most of the OECD member countries are "highly developed, democratic states." A study of the 35 OECD member nations' most recent nationwide elections found the United States of America in "28th" place.

In a US capitalist-exceptionalist or exceptionalist-capitalist mentality, leaders vehemently reject "the idea that economic and social rights are full-fledged human rights" despite the fact that, on paper, the United States recognizes the Convention on the Elimination of All Forms of Racial Discrimination and the Universal Declaration of Human Rights. US leaders have insisted that other countries respect such treaties and conventions; the US, exceptionally, violates them. While international human rights law recognizes a right to education, a right to healthcare, a right to social protection for those in need, and a right to an adequate standard of living, the United States stands alone "among developed countries in insisting that while human rights are of fundamental importance, they *do not include rights that guard against dying of hunger, dying from a lack of access to affordable healthcare, or growing up in a context of total deprivation*" (emphasis added).

Public officials' selfish ideology and negligence and a nation without value for its people and their essential contribution to government and society sow seeds of distrust among the people and cause citizens' withdrawal from feeling they have a stake in government of, by, and for them.

US Jobs of Mass Destruction

The forty-fifth US president, in his first State of the Union speech, promised jobs of the kind that are known to kill, maim, and otherwise harm the health of human beings and the natural environment—jobs of mass destruction! He promoted the nuclear industry of a country already leading the world in nuclear weaponry and the only nation to have dropped a nuclear bomb. He promoted fossil fuel and muscle cars, steel and coal. The president missed the opportunity to move the nation forward with new and forward-looking innovative jobs, jobs of new creations and that inspire creation, jobs of peace and nonviolence. Why is a bomb factory more valuable than a school of foreign language translators and promoters of cultural understanding? There is no reason it should be this way. For the sake of discussion, if we believe that value is equated with currency (money) or level of income, why not pay a translator or teacher of languages the same or more than a bomb maker? Why is a mercenary of more value than a health worker?

Remove corruption, the phenomena of pandering politics, and politicians who pander to their war industry buddies and Saudi princes, then we can reimagine, reeducate, and instill a nonviolent notion or ethos of value. Yes, people need work, decent work, living-wage work. They need valuable work that is far more than adjunct and contract work, gig work, temping, Macs and marts, and war. If a child or young person can be taught to lock and load a lethal weapon or send a remote bomb to a foreign village, a child or young man or woman can also be taught the meaningful lifelong work of playing a violin, an oboe, a snare drum, or a horn, of creating art on canvas or in clay. What happened to school music and art and nonviolent (no American football), noncompetitive physical education? When did individual school student populations become factories of thousands with disproportionately numbered, understaffed, underprepared and under supported teaching faculty members; unfit, ill prepared or inappropriately assigned counselors and administrators; absent or inadequate parental connection, care and oversight; and totally out of place armed personnel?

If a factory job engages in the manufacture of objects or fabrics, the skill, care, and product produced gives the worker a sense of satisfaction. A tailor making or mending garments of one kind or another, when done with mastery and perfection, lends a sense of satisfaction. Aside from any monetary terms or return, the work process, if meaningfully engaging work, is its own reward. There is no meaningful reward or human connection in mindlessly peering into a miniature "unsmart" electronic gadget. Robots aside, human beings as human beings need a sense of worth in work and often community in work.

The valuing of peaceful construction builds, uplifts, maintains, and adds on. It mends and amends, instead of discarding. It examines and finds a way. Peace-valued work mends broken houses (and schools), boarded-up buildings, and broken lives, and it continually adds to the store of instruments and learning. Care homes do not discard people on the streets but enable them to live independent lives *without* pharmaceutical maintenance in dens contracting drug-peddling physicians, procedures, and surgeons. Physicians are taught to leave their computer screens and actually go out into the world and heal the sick.

Reimagining, reordering, and rethinking the nature of life and work in the arena of foreign affairs could mean that groups of individuals are brought together with other cultures and language speakers and taught dialects and languages, cultures, translation, nonviolent human engagement. Their work then takes them to places—not as white- or blue-helmeted carriers of arms, lethal keepers of peace or provocateurs, but as makers of peace within the context and attitude of community.

The politicians' rationale for promoting bloodletting jobs is security, an emotional trigger. Who doesn't want to protect his or her home or country? But our nation is not under threat, and the destruction of other people and nations does not secure a belligerent nation. What it does is provide further justification for killing: "We came after them, they are coming after us, so we must increase our arsenals and combatants of violence against them." War justifies war and makes endless war endless. But if we can cultivate war makers and promote jobs making war material and selling arms, we can also promote and provide for jobs doing mediation, negotiation, and translation, and jobs teaching these skills. Imaginative change for the good is unbounded and regenerative. The choice is rooted in values, matters of character. Remove military and police presence from schools of the young, and from an early age, teach the young to value differently, to choose differently, and to discipline oneself as an act of freedom.

No human being free of propagandistic manipulation or otherwise in his or her right mind believes that killing people is decent work, good work, meaningful work, gratifying work.

If we look closely, we can see in every sector, segment, and community of American society the walking wounded—from the boardrooms to the casinos to the schoolyards or corridors to the streets. Something underlies the breakout of aggression, domestic or foreign. Government officials' deliberate blindness to and neglect of veterans' aggression (during and after deployment, even killing from a drone computer terminal in a distant place) and their neglect of the homeless, the discarded, and the abused has consequences. We must set different priorities and value differently. Responsible people with imagination can see cause and bring about cures, can heal instead of prolonging disease to increase capital, can build and rebuild, can create and recreate a far better society at home and abroad.

> The point of nonviolence is to build a floor, a strong new floor, beneath which we can no longer sink. A platform which stands a few feet above napalm, torture, exploitation, poison gas, A and H bombs. (American folk singer, songwriter, musician, and activist Joan Chandos Baez)

SOLUTIONS IN SOCIETY

FOR CONSIDERATION:
Mindfulness, Sensibility

WE ARE ONE society: an enduring, cooperating, interactive, reciprocal construct of peoples with similar and dissimilar, common and uncommon traditions, institutions, activities, and interests. Not group thinkers, but people linked by common concerns that reach beyond the self to the whole of nature. Society's wholeness, health, and survival are dependent on the talent, self-discipline, care, responsibility, and stewardship of all its members. Yes, I am an idealist. America's twenty-eighth president (1913–1921) was called an idealist and is quoted saying, "Sometimes people call me an idealist. Well, that is the way I know I am an American. America is the only [well, not the *only*] idealistic nation in the world" (Woodrow Wilson, September 8, 1919). I presume none of Wilson's power or level of pontification. Nevertheless, in the construct of society as I imagine it, any notion of freedom must have constraints if *all* are to be free.

IV

Freedom Checked by Society

Freedom and constraint are two aspects of the same necessity.
—Eighteenth-century philosopher, writer,
composer Jean-Jacques Rousseau
(June 28, 1712–July 2, 1778)

THE PARADOX HOLDS. We must see ourselves as ourselves and as a society of global dimensions. We are one of many and, in our differences, one with the whole. Freed from pandering politics, propaganda, and the prison of jingoism, we are open to seeing more clearly and honestly, living cleanly and contributively within a universal and reciprocative environment. "In civilized society we all depend upon each other and our happiness is very much owing to the good opinion of mankind," penned the English writer Samuel Johnson (1709–1784). I am sure Johnson's "good opinion of mankind" referred to something far more substantive than the twenty-first century's "liking" friends on social media.

More than "Me and Mine"

"The very idea of freedom presupposes some objective moral law which overarches rulers and ruled alike." The British author and scholar C. S. Lewis said, "We and our rulers are of one kind only so long as we are subject to one law. But if there is no Law of Nature, the ethos of any society is the creation of its rulers, educators and conditioners; and every creator stands above and outside his creation."

Politicians or men and women in public office who believe genuinely in basic moral values, the proof being in their actions (*they are what they do*), also respect and value those who solicit their votes, using criteria other than passing fancy or fashion. In reality, today's politicians respect neither the public nor themselves nor the office they hold, and the public respects neither them nor their office. Entrenched corruption has brought us to this place. We need only listen to the level of language, the incivility of debate, on a dais, on camera or news anchor chairs and roundtables, in the corridors of power, bylined or anonymous. Lewis suggested that the body politic, people more generally, "return to the crude and nursery-like belief in objective values" and, having done so, "demand of our rulers" (politicians, heads of state, public officials) more than vision, personality, or presidential posture—but the rare and most useful qualities of "virtue, knowledge, diligence and skill." We would do well to demand this of ourselves as well. Emphasizing his point, Lewis says,

> Give me a man who will do a day's work for a day's pay, who will refuse bribes, who will not make up his facts, and who has learned his job.

Fairness Principle

In the good society, the requisite attributes of diligence, skill, knowledge, and a day's work for a day's pay must be coupled with principles of shared existence and decency and fairness. Fairness means decent work and living wages, protection from predators not only of a sexual nature but those who steal earnings.

Fairness means protection from labor infractions that exceed reasonable hours of work, whether in factories or in hospital emergency rooms; protection from harmful material and equipment; and proper attire to protect from accidents and varieties of hazards. Fairness means redress and retraining. As a worker owes fair work, an employer owes fair conditions and fair wages for work. It is as unfair for a worker to show up late for work or be absent from work without notification as it is for owners, employers, supervisors, managers, and others in positions of authority to intimidate, harass, overburden, and underpay workers, whether the workers are migrant farmers, schoolteachers, construction workers, housekeepers, retail clerks, cleaners, or maintenance workers. No human being is innately more or less worthy than another. Labor unions may help ensure fairness in work assuming—*and this is doubtful*—that they are not part of the cult of pandering politics. It is an essential job of representative government to balance the scales, to ensure fairness. British politician and author David Marquand was reflecting on the imbalance in 2010 when he observed that prosperity and growth are not achieved by "the unhindered pursuit of individual self interest," or there would be no chronic poverty, indignity, cruelty, and injustice; therefore, the power of the State, "used cautiously," he warned, must participate in alleviating problems that make for an unhealthy society—poverty, indignity, cruelty, injustice. Toward this end, it is also necessary to enlist the work of authorities that transcend national boundaries, Marquand said, "Supranational institutions have to play a part."

In all fairness and common sense, robots are no substitute for the imperative of work by human beings and the human requirement of the *community* of work. The State must intercede to ensure that advanced technology does not exceed its boundaries or infringe on or erase either nature's or humanity's essentials. Common sense must not be sacrificed to profiteers' artificial intelligence. The cause of today's "unemployment and poverty," Muffy Sunde wrote in the April 2017 edition of *Freedom Socialist Voice of Revolutionary Feminism*, "is that the products of our labor are controlled by a class that does no labor." Over a decade and a half, the combination of "cheaper labor, trade agreements, and automation together in China, Mexico and other countries" has ravaged "U.S. manufacturing, particularly textiles and apparel," Sunde says.

The widening use and abuse of automation, robots, in workplaces onshore and offshore causes job loss, worker displacement, deepening poverty and inequality, and further destruction of communities, neighborhoods, families, whole societies, and indeed the welfare and potential of the whole country and its people. Sunde's suggested alternatives include "inventive workers" creating "automation that is beneficial":

- "Workers' economy [deciding] what to produce and when—without destroying human beings and the environment"
- "Computers and robots . . . used to improve the quality of life"
- "A globally collaborative working class [deciding] to junk armaments factories and build schools, quality mass housing, libraries"
- "Mass transit instead of robot bombs"
- "[Implementation of] safe, environmentally-sane agriculture concerned more with producing good-quality food than increasing speed of production"

- "Science workers focused on how to prevent and cure disease, how to clean up nuclear waste and improve the quality of Earth's food, water and air"
- "Workers in control recognizing that national borders hinder quality of life, open borders encourage the sharing of knowledge and culture, and technology"

Speaking of ideals and idealism—the American journalist, Walter Lippmann, wrote, "Ideals are an imaginative understanding of that which is desirable in that which is possible."

On Labor Day 2015, the news source TeleSUR published an appraisal of labor and the prevailing economic model and concluded that "the macroeconomic policies of the past decades have downgraded the meaning of decent work." Labor is not and should not be treated as a commodity as it is under the current model, the article said, wherein work is considered "a production cost that must be kept as low as possible to raise competitiveness and profits" and workers are cast as "*consumers* of all sorts of *loans* [emphasis added] rather than as having a legitimate share through wages in the wealth" they help create. In its ten facts about International Workers' Day, the piece suggested that what is needed is

- a new leadership "fired by human values" respecting "the dignity of work and workers,"
- leadership that moves countries "to a fairer, greener and more sustainable globalization capable of meeting people's aspirations for a decent life," and
- a model aimed at increasing the general well-being of people and reducing inequalities and that measures success not by the percentage of growth in gross domestic product (GDP) but "by the number of good-quality jobs generated"—a different kind of growth "that is environmentally conscious and focused on people."

Sharing Principle

No one wants our condescending charity. But every child knows the unfairness of taking more than one's share. Society's healthy functioning is about more than "me and mine," consuming and often wasting as much as I can. US leaders' mantras of "us and ours," "rape the land," "plunder the people," "wall the borders," and "confound the facts" full speed ahead is dead wrong. With others, we are part of a whole—not the whole.

Pacific islanders of Palau, Guam, and the Northern Mariana Islands and in the Federated States of Micronesia (the Caroline Islands), Nauru, and the Marshall Islands to Kiribati, native people are threatened with rapidly rising waters and the loss of their homes and cultures. In New York City and Middle River, Maryland, people are losing their homes to financial wizards' games of acquiring and dumping land and buildings.

In the United States, there is a "scarcity of affordable housing," according to the National Alliance to End Homelessness's 2016 report. The fewer the affordable homes, the higher the rate of homelessness. Across the United States in 2014, 1.49 million people had to use homeless shelters. On any given night in January 2016 in the United States, 549,928 people were homeless: 194,716 in families and 355,212 alone. These people had been living on the streets in cars, in homeless shelters, or in subsidized transitional housing. Almost a fourth of them were eighteen years old or younger. According to a Reuters report, in 2015, Los Angeles, Seattle, Portland, Oregon, and Hawaii "declared emergencies over the rise of homelessness."

And while hundreds of thousands of American men, women, and children were being pushed to the streets for being unable to find a permanent dwelling they could afford, real estate mogul Jared Kushner was stacking up record-breaking land deals. This son of a man convicted in 2004 on charges of tax evasion, illegal campaign donations, and witness tampering was busy dealing land.

> *2007.* Purchased the office building at 666 Fifth Avenue, New York City, "for a then-record price of $1.8 billion [most borrowed]."

> *2008 (property crash period).* "Dumped the property" at a selling price (the retail portion) exceeding $1 billion.

> *August 18, 2014 (with partners).* "Acquired a three-building apartment portfolio in Middle River, Maryland, for $37.9 million."

2013–2014 (with his company). "Acquired more than 11,000 units throughout the New York, New Jersey, and Baltimore."

May 2015. "Purchased 50.1 percent of the Times Square Building from Africa Israel Investments Ltd. for $295 million."

As of 2017, part of Jared Corey Kushner's biography read, "senior advisor to his father-in-law, U.S. President Donald Trump," as well as being "an American real estate investor and developer, and publisher" (Wikipedia).

The RT program "Renegade" reported in its April 2017 edition on the issue of land-grabbers and those who suffer the loss. Land is essential for human existence and the original source of all wealth, "yet bankers, economists, and politicians have simplistically lumped land and capital together" with the dire consequence of shoving ordinary people to the grate. Across the world, people's land "is being stolen from them."

Ethics Principle: Do No Harm

If the religions text to which a person subscribes or says he believes says don't steal, kill, lie, harass, or envy, why do these things? Unless, of course, one does not really believe what he says he believes, or he believes that saying or preaching to others fulfills the ethic. I don't subscribe to that philosophy. I believe we are what we do, and if we say we are ethical, that we believe, for example, in doing no harm, then think about it and, to the best of your ability, do no harm. The Christians' text contains something called The Great Commission, and if this means anything at all in contemporary times, it must surely mean to let one's own character shine through in *good* behavior. If one wants to teach goodness, be good; don't lecture other people about a subjective notion of good (or god or democracy, for that matter). Don't preach religious texts while committing and aiding and abetting conflict, war, and social unrest at home and abroad. It is possible that if all the people demanding "Merry *Christmas*" instead of "Happy Holidays" or preaching biblical texts on radio or sending "prayers and thoughts" to the selective dead people and their survivors—if they were practicing Christians, there would be no wars or mass killing at home or abroad.

Love is a very complex, subjectively driven, variously defined and understood concept. And for this reason, love may be impossible for most people to have or to show for the rest of the people. But in the least, we can manage respect for other human beings as human beings (other nations and cultures) to the extent of never lifting a hand or weapon or causing a hand or weapon to be lifted against them—unless in absolutely clear, indisputable cases of self-defense, not expedient pretexts pandering to special interests.

If one does not believe the science, it is far better to err on the side of preservation than on the side of annihilation. This is particularly critical when facing that which we can neither create nor recreate.

Contrary to the cult of panderers who are too lazy to imagine and plan a different future or who prefer the easy old road and their take and kickback, the evidence of environmental harm and causation is beyond doubt. In 2017, the Union of Concerned Scientists again raised the alarm about environmental damage, repeating what had been covered in some press accounts: that fossil fuel companies had not only been aware for a long time that their products were causing global warming (as the tobacco industry knew about their products causing cancer) but, with politicians' wink and nod, had continued and even increased their harm to the environment. In the period 1880–1980, greenhouse emissions traced to "the largest 90 carbon producers" had contributed 57 percent of the "observed rise in atmospheric carbon dioxide" and "nearly 50 percent of the rise in the global average temperature." In the period 1980–2010, emissions reportedly were traced to fifty companies that contributed an estimated "10 percent of the global average temperature increase" and an estimated "4 percent of sea level rise."

The 2017 report said that among the fifty high emissions, "investor-owned carbon producers" were well-known companies such as BP, Chevron, ConocoPhillips, ExxonMobil, Peabody, and Shell. The whole group was responsible for "16 percent [est.] of the global average temperature increase" and "11 percent [est.] of the global sea level rise" in the 1880–2010 period.

A character of greed, selfishness, and terminal arrogance binds deniers to their false philosophy, which stands in the way of doing what is right for all—from Pacific islanders to nomads of Africa and South America to India's farmers to the Louisiana Gulf's fishermen. Preservation of society is essential to the ecosystem, the balance of nature, to human beings' lives, and basic livelihoods. C. S. Lewis pointed to "greed and pride" as causes of "misery and vice," and at times, conditions are worsened by holding on to a "false philosophy."

Society is universal, reciprocative, and indispensable. It is the duty of those who inhabit it—especially as we can neither create nor recreate it—to care for it, protect it, honor it, and preserve it. Within the constraints of the "social contract," said French political philosopher Jean-Jacques Rousseau, human beings give and receive.

Contemporary writer Dr. Vandana Shiva is a physicist credentialed in the philosophy of science (PhD), an author of twenty books, a lecturer, and an environmental activist who has contributed intellectually and through activist campaigns to fields such as intellectual property rights, biodiversity, biotechnology, bioethics, and genetic engineering. In 1987, she founded the Research Foundation for Science, Technology and Ecology, which led to the 1991 creation of a national movement to protect the diversity and integrity of living resources, especially native seed, the promotion of organic farming and fair trade (Navdanya). She has also assisted grassroots organizations of the Green Movement in Africa, Asia, Latin America, Ireland, Switzerland, and Austria with campaigns against genetic engineering.

In a 2014 interview, Dr. Shiva made these alarming statements: Climate change is "a corporate-driven industry which has dismantled our processes of people's rights, democratic rights, and the cultures that have protected our ecosystems." Moreover, she said, "there is a continuum between wars we see as wars," such as what's happening in Syria. But there are also "the wars against the planet and the wars against people. . . . As Wall Street makes the world's economies collapse, the only economy left is war."

V

Pandering Politics and Divisive Isms

Promoters of identify politics, political partisans posturing as "popular opponents" of a perceived "right-wing" are continuing a "decades' long clever pageantry of divide, distract, and do nothing substantive."

—World Socialist Web Site columnist Tom Hall
"The political issues behind the removal of
Confederate monuments in New Orleans"
(Quote with minor edits)

THE ISMS OF race, sex, and other sectarian or separatist notions distract, divide, weaken, and ultimately destroy the essential whole. Increased round-the-clock media and government propaganda, fearmongering, and pressure to consent create division in the population, "a classic divide-and-conquer tactic."

Powerful partisans, media, and partners "want to divide us—whoever we are with our nationalities, classes, ages, identities, genders, backgrounds, and more." They want all of us "to squabble, fight, hate, and eat each other to deflect our energies from the real sources behind the social, political, and economic problems besieging" the country. "They want you to hate your neighbor, curse your friend, and compete for resources, while continually denying and eroding the most basic of rights and infrastructure owed to you—[all] under the guise of security, fighting terrorism, and stability." The writer, Yazan al-Saadi, was writing of a country in the Middle East, but it sounds very much like the state of affairs in the United States of America.

When people making up a huge sector of socioeconomic class separate themselves into camps of hostility and when other classes subsist on distracting and containing the masses in lower socioeconomic classes, the body politic is severely weakened, perhaps fatally wounded. When politicians, on the one hand, pander to inordinate power and, on the other, pacify the masses by pandering expediently to their isms of class, color, race, creed, national origin, sex, and innumerable fragmentations or mutations, all of these classes, groups and fragments, fighting among themselves, render any idealized notion of governance of, by and for, or representative of all people impossible. Society breaks down. The whole disintegrates. Progress, constructive change, and evolution—maturity, spiritual and psychological evolution—of the species cannot happen in this atmosphere. Perhaps that is the outcome intended by some and unintended by others.

Progress How Far

War broke out everywhere, rising like fire from the earth. People's lands were stolen from them; the men were forced to wander the earth, and the women were subjected to unspeakable acts. The country receded into wilderness conditions. Hundreds of thousands went to war, believing they were saving their way of life. Wealthy "patriots" stayed home. War dead totaled in the hundreds of thousands, and those who returned reaped their rewards in poverty and deepening division—both sides of the divided people languished "without land, property, or hope for economic gains." The author was describing conditions in nineteenth-century America, conditions that, to a significant degree, have returned or have hung on in twenty-first century America because we have failed to hear and heed lessons of the past. The old strategies of false patriotism, profit, poverty, and pandering persist seemingly as standing policy; and modern masses vacuously finger their gadgets, *face time* their "friends," embrace debt slavery and DNA and appear in television commercials foolishly touting snake oil as proof of their "tribal ancestry."

Identity or tribal politics cages some and institutionalizes incestuous corruption and incompetence in others. Isms promoted by such professional racialists as Michael Eric Dyson, golden boy of some establishment media and op-ed writer with the inordinately powerful *New York Times*, entrenches victimhood by reinforcing what he terms an "unbridgeable racial divide in America" and, in Patrick Martin's words, reducing "legitimate anger" to racialist narratives that end in "expressions of demoralized helplessness." Forever enslaved! Forever victim to and forever dependent on Dyson-esque charity, champions, exploiters, and victimizers!

"Self-serving 'racialization' of reality" defeats the purpose of progress. Perpetuated by mainstream newspaper reporting and such hysterical sound bites as "black lives matter" and "white lives matter most" and sundry backlash, more violence, and use of force by law enforcement officers become "race wars" and variations on a color-coding theme. But as Martin reports, from outside mainstream media, 2015 recorded more than 500 white people dying "after encounters with police." In the first seven months of 2016, another 200–300 white people died in these kinds of encounters. The "ruling class," regardless of color, Martin opines, relies on the "promotion of racialist politics to divide the working class and divert the anger among youth and workers into a blind alley." The solution, he says, is "to denounce . . . racialist lies and fight for solidarity" with working classes of any group, regardless of race, color, culture, or immigrant status.

Bridge Forward

Contrary to present performance, the civil rights movement accurately documented in US history involved major programs of social reform and improvements in the social conditions of the whole working class. The twenty-first century display, in David Walsh's words, is no more than "a self-centered project driven by a 'pseudo-left' and an 'upper-middle-class' obsession with race, gender and sexual identity." America's great and expanding gulf, particularly fissured in the camp of the masses, "is evident in the poorer and lower socioeconomic groups' ongoing hostilities, scratching for survival." The internal struggle among the richest is "far removed from the needs of the working class" and devoid of "democratic" or "progressive" voice. The "richest 5 to 10 percent" group's "shrill demands" manifest their own battle among themselves.

A truly progressive course would be to repudiate "racialist and nationalist filth promulgated" by political parties and "those who orbit around bourgeois politics," David Walsh wrote.

In a better world in which public officials abstained from pandering, pacifying, and placating tribal fragments or other selfishly vested interests—playing one against the other—for personal gain, there would be an overall healthy society. The masses of people may not achieve a mythical dream, but then no one who is truly awake and aware aspires to a dream. What all people would have is *enough*. And toward that end, adding to Patrick Martin's and

David Walsh's thoughts, it is the responsibility of all people to forego the isms and xenophobic diatribes, DNA worship, and war, and to begin to work in solidarity with one another across characteristics such as race, color, culture, creed, gender, and immigrant status. If we seek something more than fear, division, paralysis, and anxieties, again paraphrasing some of Yazan al-Saadi's words, "the best approach is to hold on, hold on and have solidarity," empathy, humanity—with the refugee and the soldier, the migrant worker and the daily laborer, the youth and the elders, the activist and the citizen, those within and outside national borders. Concerned solidarity is "a vital, radical, powerful act" in these troubled times. We cannot allow our solidarity to be broken "because with solidarity" and shared concern, "all is not lost."

VI

"Regime Change" Variation on the Theme of Violence

When a whole country is unjustly overrun and conquered by a foreign army and subjected to military law . . . it is not too soon for honest [people] to rebel and revolutionize. . . . This duty [is] the more urgent [because] . . . the country so overrun is not our own. . . . Ours is the invading army.

—American poet and essayist
Henry David Thoreau (1817–1862)
"Civil Disobedience," 1849
(Quote with minor edits)

DOES ANYONE HONESTLY believe that one nation has a right to take what belongs to other nations and, more often than not, take it by force? Does anyone believe that such action is either legal or moral? Does anyone honestly believe that powerful nations of the world, through the actions and policies of their leaders, down through the centuries up through the present day, should be allowed to effectively, factually, and metaphorically get away with murder—destroy the lives, places, cultures, and futures of peoples and nations of the world over and over again? Does anyone believe that any pretext, any excuse, any expediency sufficiently justifies either the act of aggression in the first instance or the failure to prosecute in the second instance? Is this the legacy an honorable nation, a *good* nation, leaves to its young, a legacy set before the world as a noble example to all peoples and nations?

My answer to all these questions is no, and in the realms of international and domestic affairs, any change worth the name would have to reverse the current trend and uproot the entrenched pattern of lawlessness and the unconscionable acts and policies of inordinately powerful, nuclear-threatening, selfish super-powered nations and their leaders.

To ordinary people, it would seem obvious that change, reform, transformation begins at home and that its course should be thoughtful and nonviolent. Violence calls to violence. We have seen this pattern played out repeatedly in domestic and foreign relations: violence causes violence.

In the United States, one administration promises change as a reset of policies and approach in international relations. Another promises to "clean the swamp," clear out the old guard in Washington. Both gave the world endless foreign wars, regime change, threats, displacement, destabilization, and violence in actions and words. US representatives at the United Nations outdid themselves in belligerence, ignorance, incompetence, recklessness, rudeness, and all-around disrespect of nations.

For the past several years, the only change Americans and the world have become accustomed to, unfortunately, is US leadership's televised, even bragging, policies and practice of removing foreign leaders and heads of state from office, often killing them or having them killed, and destroying the lives and customs and places—creating massive displacement and disease— of thousands of the world's peoples. These acts are in direct violation of international covenants to which the United States is signatory. Critically at issue is the UN Charter. After World War II, in 1945 the United States ratified the United Nations Charter, the preeminent international law document legally binding the US government to the Charter's provisions, including Article 2(4), which prohibits the threat or use of force in international relations, except in very limited circumstances. This means one nation cannot willy-nilly or cavalierly remove another country's head of state. Any legal claim advanced to justify regime change by a foreign power "carries a particularly heavy burden." And yet, almost before the ink was dry, the US began a tyranny of regime change.

David Harrison calls it hubris and self-elevation that drives US leaders to repeatedly breach the sovereignty of other countries while walling in its own righteous sovereignty. In the name of a delusional divine right, Americans, since World War II, have interfered in "dozens and dozens of sovereign states" to bring about regime change. Using false justifications or pretexts, "they have caused civil wars, assassinated leaders, eradicated opposition members, and murdered thousands of innocent people—millions in Korea and Vietnam," David Harrison wrote. "Yet they [USA! USA! USA!] . . . see themselves as honest, honorable human beings."

After World War II, the US government extended its "backyard" Latin and Caribbean regime change aggression to Korea (1950–1953), Iran (1953 coup d'état), Cuba (1961), Vietnam (1954–1975), Argentina (1976–1983), and other operations throughout the world.

In a long train of abuses and the callous shedding of blood, through overt and covert operations, violent alliances, government overthrow, and out-and-out war, the United States has terrorized the world, plundered nations' natural resources, slaughtered its people, and stymied advancements that would have served basic human needs. Some of the examples of the United States' breach of sovereignty, violation of the peace, and war on humanity (thirty-four countries listed alphabetically, often multiple invasions of or covert operations in a single country) reaching back to the early post-WWII period into the present day are these:

- **Afghanistan:** (covert op, 1979–1989) Afghanistan, Operation Cyclone; (US v. Soviets, 1989–1992), US alliance with the mujahideen, a movement of religious students, the Taliban (var. al-Qaeda); (1996–2001) well-funded Islamists led by an exiled Saudi Arabian, Osama bin Laden (reportedly killed by US forces on May 2, 2011, in Pakistan, and buried at sea); (2001–) continuing US aggression and occupation; (2003) Afghan paramilitary, politician and warlord, Gulbuddin Hekmatyar, twice-engaged in regime change with the aid of the United States (early 1990s, early 2000s), described by his countrymen as "Butcher of Kabul" for having contributed to the deaths of at least 50,000 civilians in Kabul alone in the early 1990s, in 2003 is US designated "global terrorist."
- **Albania:** (covert op, 1949–1953) Albania
- **Bolivia:** (covert op, 1964) Bolivian coup d'état; (1967) Bolivia, Che Guevara, revolutionary leader—CIA-organized military operation ended in his capture and execution by the Bolivian Army; (covert op, 1971) Bolivian coup d'état
- **Brazil:** (covert op, 1964) Brazilian coup d'état
- **Cambodia:** (1959) Cambodia, Norodom Sihanouk, leader; (1963) again; (1969) again
- **Chile:** (covert op, 1970–1973) Chile; (1970) Chile, General Rene Schneider, commander in chief of army; (1970) Chile, Salvador Allende, president—unsuccessful US-supported coup, Project FUBELT; (1976) Chile, exiled Chilean foreign minister Orlando

Letelier—blown up in Washington, DC, as part of Operation Condor with at least tacit US support

- **China:** (1950s) China, Prime Minister Chou En-lai—several attempts on his life
- **Congo:** (covert op, 1960) Congo coup d'état; (June 1960) Patrice Lumumba became the Congo's first prime minister after independence from Belgium, was dismissed in September at the instigation of the United States, and in January 1961, was assassinated at the request of Dwight Eisenhower; several years of civil conflict and chaos, CIA backed deposing of President Joseph Kasavubu (statesman and first president of the independent Congo republic from 1960 to 1965, Joseph Kasavubu had shortly after independence in 1960 ousted the Congo's first premier, Patrice Lumumba, after the breakdown of order in the country); (1965) ascension to power by CIA-linked Mobutu Sese Seko, who ruled and robbed the country for more than thirty years (a kleptocracy) while the Zairian people lived in abject poverty
- **Costa Rica:** (1950s–1970s) Costa Rica, José Figueres, president—two attempts on his life
- **Cuba:** (covert op, 1961) Cuba, Bay of Pigs Invasion; (1960s–1970s) Cuba, Fidel Castro, president—many attempts on his life, including poisoned cigars
- **Dominican Republic:** (1961) Dominican Republic, General Rafael Trujillo, dictator since 1930—shot dead; (1965) Dominican Republic, Francisco Caamaño, opposition leader
- **Egypt:** (1957) Egypt, Gamal Abdel Nasser, president
- **Germany:** (1950s) Germany, CIA/neo-Nazi hit list of more than two hundred political figures in West Germany to be "put out of the way" in the event of a Soviet invasion
- **Ghana:** (covert op, 1966) Ghana, coup d'état
- **Guatemala:** (covert op, 1954) Guatemalan coup d'état
- **Haiti:** (1961) Haiti, François "Papa Doc" Duvalier, leader
- **India:** (1955) India, Jawaharlal Nehru, prime minister
- **Indonesia:** (1950s, 1962) Indonesia, Sukarno, president; (covert op, 1957–1958) Indonesian coup d'état
- **Iraq:** (1960) Iraq, Brigadier General Abdul Karim Kassem, leader; (1963) Iraq, CIA supports the Ba'athists, including Saddam Hussein, in a coup in Iraq against the Qassim government; (1991) Iraq, Saddam

Hussein, leader—attempt to kill him; (2003) Saddam Hussein and his two sons—two killings and a semijudicial execution; (2003–) US war ongoing

- **Iran:** (1951) Iran, Mohammed Mossadegh, prime minister; (covert op, 1953) Iranian coup d'état; (1982) Iran, Ayatollah Khomeini, leader; (covert op, 1996) Iraq, coup attempt
- **Jamaica:** (1976) Jamaica, Michael Manley, prime minister
- **Korea:** (1949) Korea, Kim Koo, opposition leader; (1951) North Korea, Kim Il Sung, premier
- **Lebanon:** (1985) Lebanon, Sheikh Mohammed Hussein Fadlallah, Shiite leader—eighty people killed in the attempt
- **Libya:** (1980–1986) Libya, Muammar al-Qaddafi, leader—several plots and attempts on his life; (covert op, 2011) Libyan civil war
- **Nicaragua:** (covert op, 1981–1987) Nicaragua, Contras; (1983) Nicaragua, Miguel d'Escoto, foreign minister; (1983) Morocco, General Ahmed Dlimi, army; (1984) Nicaragua, the nine commandants of the Sandinista National Directorate
- **Panama:** (1970s, 1981) Panama, General Omar Torrijos, leader; (1972) Panama, General Manuel Noriega, chief of intelligence—captured alive and been imprisoned ever since
- **Philippines:** (black op, poison, 1957, 1960) Filipino opposition leader, statesman, jurist, poet, Claro Mayo Recto Jr., in public office 1931-1960; (1957) campaigning against US military bases in the Philippines, US Central Intelligence Agency conducted black propaganda operations against him; (October 2, 1960) died while on a cultural mission in Europe; before sustaining a "heart attack," Recto had "met with two mysterious Caucasians wearing business suits"; CIA suspected of killing him. US government documents later revealed that, years earlier, CIA station chief Ralph Lovett and US ambassador to the Philippines Raymond Spruance had discussed killing Recto "with a vial of poison."
- **Somalia:** (1993) Somalia, Mohamed Farah Aidid, prominent clan leader—failed attempt, but he died later
- **Syria:** (covert op, 1949) Syrian coup d'état; (covert op, 1956–1957) Syria, crisis; (covert op, 2011–) Syria
- **Tibet:** (covert op, 1951–1956) Tibet
- **Turkey:** (covert op, 1980) Turkish coup d'état

- **Vietnam (South):** (covert coup, 1963) South Vietnam, Ngo Dinh Diem, president—successful attempt to replace one puppet leader with another
- **Yemen:** (2017) "US launched 20 airstrikes in Yemen since late February: Pentagon" (PressTV, reporting April 4, 2017)
- **Zaire (now Democratic Republic of Congo):** (1961) Zaire; (1965) Zaire, president overthrown and replaced by Mobutu Sese Seko (further reference: 1961 deposing of Patrice Lumumba); (1975) Zaire, Mobutu Sese Seko, president—seized power in 1965 coup

Violent aggression exacts costs. The Delphi Initiative is a group of intellectuals, mainly but not exclusively European, who proclaim their opposition to "an international policy of War." According to their website, they "reject a new 'Cold War' against Russia (or China)." They reject "the very Hot War against the Arab and Muslim world," and they "oppose the culmination of [these] into the War against Nature, organized by big international corporations, international Finance and many governments and states controlled by them."

Delphi is well aware that foreign interventions and breaches of nations' sovereignty have far-reaching consequences that often ricochet. US interventions, particularly in the Middle East, have led "not only to the nearly complete destruction of a number of important states of this region," authors at the Delphi Initiative write, "but they have also provoked a serious refugee crisis and 'terrorist' attacks in Europe." The cycle, ricochet, and continuance of violence, human rights abuse, and aftereffects and shock waves take many forms: "the refugee crisis and 'terrorist' [an alphabet soup of "jihadist"] threats have come to be used as 'pretexts' [for curtailing] democratic rights of working people in Europe" and creating chaos and conflict among states, rendering them "unable to oppose 'globalization', neoliberalism and imperialism."

Casualties and Consequences: Yemen through 2017

US wars, occupation, and interference cause unbearable suffering wherever they exist, particularly to nations and peoples throughout the Middle East region. A recent case in point is Yemen, where cholera cases in 2017 were estimated to exceed 200,000 and were "increasing at an average of 5,000 a